THE HISTORY OF ACID TRIPPING

The History of Acid Tripping
Copyright© 2012 by Mikazuki Publishing House
ISBN-13: 978-1-937981-36-5

Author: Eric Hurtado

Editor: Kambiz Mostofizadeh

Publisher: Mikazuki Publishing House
www.MikazukiPublishingHouse.com

I0116079

THE HISTORY OF ACID TRIPPING

TABLE OF CONTENTS

THE HISTORY OF ACID TRIPPING

The 1960's were times of great unrest within American society; the nation was torn apart on almost every major issue of the time. The war in Vietnam caused many people to

THE HISTORY OF ACID TRIPPING

reconsider the issue of the draft, culturally the

country was experiencing a revolution in the

fields of art and music, and drugs were

quickly becoming associated with the un-

conformed youth of the time. Since the 1960's

drugs have become a sensitive issue to discuss

in our country because many people simply

assume that nothing positive can be derived

from the use of illegal substances. But to

refuse to discuss the issue of drugs is

detrimental to our society because it leaves

incomplete the history of the United States.

The purpose of this work will be to

look at just one subset of the drug culture

within American society during the 1960's.

THE HISTORY OF ACID TRIPPING

The subset I intend to look at is that of

psychedelic drugs, specifically LSD. This

paper takes as its focus the goal to reach a

conclusion about why the counter-culture of

the 1960's embraced psychedelic drugs. I plan

to accomplish this task by delving into the

history of LSD and showing how it came to be

popularized within 1960's American society. I

will do so by first exposing the origins of

LSD, from its first synthesis to its first "trip"

and the attention it received, and what the

fungus that it is derived from is historically

associated with. This is of relevance to this

work because the fungus itself is associated

with altered states of delirium. Secondly, I

THE HISTORY OF ACID TRIPPING

will look at the first experimental uses of LSD

by the psychiatric community in North

America. Thirdly, my research will concern

itself with the use of LSD by the CIA and the

Army during the Cold War Periods of the

1950's and 1960's. Finally, I will look at the

popularization of LSD. This last section will

concern itself with the use of the drug by

musicians and artists as well, as with

movements that helped to further expand the

use of the drug, like Timothy Leary's religious

use of the drug and the Merry Pranksters tour

across America.

THE HISTORY OF ACID TRIPPING

26 July 1963

MEMORANDUM FOR: Director of Central Intelligence

SUBJECT : Report of Inspection of MKULTRA

1. In connection with our survey of Technical Services Division, DD/P, it was deemed advisable to prepare the report of the MKULTRA program in one copy only, in view of its unusual sensitivity.

2. This report is forwarded herewith.

3. The MKULTRA activity is concerned with the research and development of chemical, biological, and radiological materials capable of employment in clandestine operations to control human behavior. The end products of such research are subject to very strict controls including a requirement for the personal approval of the Deputy Director/Plans for any operational use made of these end products.

4. The cryptonym MKULTRA encompasses the R&D phase and a second cryptonym MKDELTA denotes the DD/P system for control of the operational employment of such materials. The provisions of the MKULTRA authority also cover [ ] The administration and control of this latter activity were found to be generally satisfactory and are discussed in greater detail in the main body of the report on TSD.

5. MKULTRA was authorized by the then Director of Central Intelligence, Mr. Allen W. Dulles, in 1953. The TSD was assigned responsibility thereby to employ a portion of its R&D budget, eventually set at 20%, for research in behavioral materials and [ ] under purely internal and compartmented controls, (further details are provided in paragraph 3 of the attached report). Normal procedures for project approval, funding, and accounting were waived. However, special arrangements for audit of expenditures have been evolved in subsequent years.

Seri Acy 286.
185209/1

THE HISTORY OF ACID TRIPPING

LSD: Origins and first Uses

LSD was first synthesized by the

chemist Albert Hoffman for the Sandoz

pharmaceutical corporation in 1938.

Hoffmann had been working with ergot

derivatives in order to obtain a circulatory and

respiratory stimulant. The 25th substance to be

extracted from the ergot derivates was named

LSD-25, simply for laboratory identification.[1]

Ergot, *Claviceps Purpurae*, is a

dark purple fungus that infects rye.[2] In her

article, "Badiou Not on Acid", Arun Saldanha

---

[1] Albert Hoffmann, *LSD: My Problem Child*, trans.
Jonathan Ott (New York: McGraw-Hill, 1980), 12.
[2] Arun Saldanha, "The LSD Event: Badiou Not on Acid,"
Theory and Event Vol. 10, No. 4 (2007): 3, accesed
November 22, 2010. http://0-

THE HISTORY OF ACID TRIPPING

mentions, "Ergot doesn't kill the plant, but on animals, excessive consumption can have serious gangrenous and convulsive effects. The sufferer also hallucinates because the fungus blocks the blood circulation to the brain."[3]

Despite these negative properties ergot, served a useful purpose in that it was used in obstetrics from Europe to China, primarily for stopping bleeding. It also helped in both abortion and childbirth. Very early on, though, the mind-altering potency of ergot was recognized and it is even possible that the

---

muse.jhu.edu.torofind.csudh.edu/journals/theory_and_eve
nt/v010/10.4saldanha.html.
[3] Ibid, 3

THE HISTORY OF ACID TRIPPING

Greeks may have used it during the Eleusinian Mysteries, a ritual practiced in Athens over 2,000 years ago where beer made with ergot infected grains was consumed.[4] In Medieval Europe, ergot regularly infected entire communities when bakers didn't take care in selecting the grains they used to make bread. Peoples' limbs were known to become gangrenous, convulsions then occurred, progressing into insanity, and finally death.[5] The ergot poisoning eventually came to be recognized as a dancing mania on the European continent, as people were

---

[4] Martin A. Lee and Bruce Shlain, *Acid Dreams: the CIA, LSD and the Sixties Rebellion* (New York: Grove Press, 1985), 66.

[5] Arun Saldanha, "The LSD Event," 3.

THE HISTORY OF ACID TRIPPING

known to dance frenetically in the streets

THE HISTORY OF
ACID TRIPPING

while simultaneously yelling out their

visions.[6]

So Ergot, from which LSD is

synthesized, was therefore already associated

with psychoactive disturbances aside from its

use in obstetrics. It is no wonder then that

such a powerful inebriant could be derived

from this source in 1938 when Albert

Hoffmann furthered his ergot research.

---

[6] Ibid, 5

THE HISTORY OF ACID TRIPPING

Hoffman and the first trip

Contrary to popular belief, the first LSD inebriation was not too much fun for Albert Hoffmann who first consumed the drug 5 years after his first initial synthesis. In 1943, as Hoffmann puts it in his book _LSD: My Problem Child_, "A peculiar presentiment-the feeling that this substance could posses properties other than those established in the first investigations-induced me, five years after the first synthesis, to produce LSD-25 once again so that a sample could be given to the pharmacological department for further tests."[7] Somewhere in his synthesis of LSD-

---

[7] Albert Hoffmann, _LSD: My Problem Child_, 14.

THE HISTORY OF ACID TRIPPING

25, Hoffmann was exposed to the drug,

although Hoffmann could not understand how

this had happened. It more than likely was the

result of the substance being absorbed into his

body through his skin. He later goes on to

describe that he had to stop his lab work

because he felt restlessness combined with a

slight dizziness and upon arrival at his home

he began to feel the psychoactive properties of

the drug. Upon closing his eyes, Hoffmann

saw a stream of images, shapes, and colors.[8]

---

[8] Ibid, 15.

THE HISTORY OF ACID TRIPPING

This initial exposure left him with the curiosity of knowing if LSD-25 had been responsible for his experience three days earlier, so he decided that only self experimentation could give him the answer. On April 19, 1943, Hoffmann took 0.25 milligrams of LSD-25, a massive overdose by today's standards, and diluted it with some water. Hoffmann writes of the inebriation, that familiar objects and furniture within his home

THE HISTORY OF ACID TRIPPING

assumed threatening forms, and that his

neighbor from whom he'd requested some

milk turned into a malevolent witch with a

colored mask. Hoffmann had felt as if he was

possessed by a demon and that any effort he

put into stopping the dissolution of his ego

and the outer world was simply a wasted

effort.[9] Upon the arrival of a doctor to his

home Hoffmann found that his blood pressure

and breathing were normal and the doctor

found no reason to prescribe him medication,

Hoffmann's experience had been purely

mental.[10]

---

[9] Ibid, 17-18.
[10] Ibid, 18.

THE HISTORY OF ACID TRIPPING

The following day Hoffmann wrote to his superiors at Sandoz mentioning his experience the night before and, as he had expected, the first reactions to his experience were quite simply astonishment. Hoffmann's superiors phoned him immediately and asked if the dosage he had reported was correct. An active compound of such potency was simply not known to have been in existence before Hoffman's first exposure to LSD. Hoffmann's superiors repeated the experiments with a third of the dosage used in the first experiment, but the results were still extremely potent.[11] LSD-25 then had a short-

---

[11] Ibid, 21.

THE HISTORY OF ACID TRIPPING

lived trial phase in which it was tested on

animals within the Sandoz pharmaceutical

THE HISTORY OF ACID TRIPPING

department, but the experiments would

quickly be abandoned since the drug produced

mainly psychoactive effects which were quite

difficult to measure on animals. It is worth

mentioning that this research progressed

within Sandoz in the direction of finding out

how much LSD-25 could be fatal to mice and

other small creatures. The amount of LSD-25

required to kill a person has never been

discovered, because the research necessary to

this task has never been conducted.[12]

LSD and the Psychiatric Community

Soon after Sandoz ceased to

experiment with LSD on animals, the first

---

[12] Ibid, 25-26.

THE HISTORY OF ACID TRIPPING

systematic trial of the drug on humans began

at the University of Zurich. The experiments

were handled by Werner A. Stoll, who

happened to be the first psychiatrist to try

LSD and the son of Hoffmann's superior at

the Sandoz Corporation. In his experiments he

used both subjects who had been diagnosed as

schizophrenics as well as mentally stable

subjects. The results from this study were later

published, and this publication would also

include the notion that LSD could be used as a

tool for research in psychiatry because of the

psychoactive effects of LSD.[13] In the time to

---

[13] Ibid, 36.

THE HISTORY OF ACID TRIPPING

come, the psychiatric community would

debate and research LSD extensively.

The initial idea that most psychiatrists

prescribed to involved the notion that LSD

produced a "model psychosis" and could help

researchers to understand the mental

afflictions of their patients, particularly

schizophrenics. But soon psychiatrist would

THE HISTORY OF ACID TRIPPING

adopt the idea shared by Albert Hoffmann that

LSD could be used to speed up psycho-

therapy because of its tendency to cause the

ego to melt way during the peak of a trip. To

Hoffmann the drug was useful in serving this

purpose because it could help the user out of

an egocentric viewpoint, as well as to more

easily recall traumatic experiences.[14] In Albert

Hoffmann's book, _LSD: My Problem Child_,

specifications for the way that Hoffmann

intended the drug to be used are given in

detail. One of the most significant things to

note from this text is the authors'

recommendation for psychiatrist to use LSD

---

[14] Ibid, 48.

THE HISTORY OF ACID TRIPPING

in psychotherapy and to take the drug with

patients.[15]

LSD Researchers in North America

In the United States LSD was first used

in research by the psychiatrist Dr. Max Rinkel

in 1949. Dr. Rinkel organized an LSD study at

the Boston Psychopathic Institute which was

affiliated with Harvard. Rinkel tested LSD on

one hundred volunteers and concluded that the

drug, "produced a transitory psychotic

disturbance". In the process, he also proposed

that mental disorders could be studied

objectively within laboratories.[16] The research

---

[15] Ibid, see appendix, 46-48.
[16] Lee and Shlain, *Acid dreams*, 20.

THE HISTORY OF
ACID TRIPPING

history of LSD within the U.S. was as Arun

Saldanha mentions in her article, "...was

directly or indirectly connected to upholding

the American nation-state."[17] And most of the

research on LSD carried on in the U.S. had

ties to either the Army or the CIA, as we will

see in the sections to follow. Within this time

---

[17] Arun Saldanha, "The LSD Event," 27.

THE HISTORY OF ACID TRIPPING

period, there were very few researches

conducting experiments with LSD in the

United States, most of the research was being

conducted in the Saskatchewan region of

Canada, because the Canadian legal system

had much more lax laws on experimental

pharmaceuticals. As Erika Dyck puts it in her

article, "Land of the Living Sky with

Diamonds." "The emergence of psychedelic

psychiatry in Saskatchewan suggests that the

intellectual and geographical climate of

experimentation produced a set of conditions

that influenced medical research in ways that

were not experienced elsewhere."[18] But the

---

[18] Ericka Dyck, "The Land of the Living Sky with

THE HISTORY OF ACID TRIPPING

work that occurred in Canada is still relevant

to this paper because many of the figures

involved in Canadian LSD research would

later make their way down into the United

States, as was the case with Al M. Hubbard in

Vancouver and Humphrey Osmond in

Saskatchewan.

It was in Canada that Al M. Hubbard

first began using LSD to treat alcoholics,

Hubbard later ran into trouble when U.S.

medical officials complained that he was

practicing medicine without a license, but he

quickly got out of it by purchasing a PhD

Diamonds: A place for Radical Psychiatry," *Journal of Canadian Stuides* Vol. 41 No. 3 (2007): 43, accessed, November 22, 2010.
http://0muse.jhu.edu.torofind.csudh.edu/search/results?search_id=2055295640&action=reload.

THE HISTORY OF ACID TRIPPING

from a diploma mill.[19] But contrary to what

one might believe progress into LSD research

was in fact being made in Canada. Dr.

Humphrey Osmond was one of the pioneering

researchers stationed in Saskatchewan in the

1950's. His work began with research into the

effects of mescaline, derived from peyote and

similar to LSD in its psychoactive nature,

requiring larger doses to bring about more

vivid hallucinations. It was under the

influence of mescaline that Osmond first came

to the realization that he could comprehend

the psychoses of his patients.[20]

---

[19] Lee and Shlain, *Acid dreams*, 51.
[20] Dyck, "The Land of the Living Sky," 53.

THE HISTORY OF ACID TRIPPING

Osmond soon went into LSD research because, to the liking of his superiors, the drug was more readily available thanks to the Sandoz Corporation and also much more cost effective than mescaline. The Saskatchewan researchers did indeed make progress with LSD therapy and one of their main successes had to do with alcoholics. Psychiatrists using LSD therapy attempted to treat alcoholics and they had high rates of success; they argued that over 50% of their patients made a full recovery from alcoholism, making it one of the most effective ways to treat alcohol-ism at the time.[21] The researchers argued that an

---

[21] ibid 56

THE HISTORY OF ACID TRIPPING

alcoholic's tendency to resist intervention would be overcome once delirium tremens, a stage in alcohol recovery usually associated with hitting rock bottom, set in, but this could be dangerous because that stage of alcoholism can lead to death. LSD was a wonderful drug because it offered the possibility of mentally experiencing delirium tremens without the physical damage that was part of the stage, in doing so, the treatment of alcoholism was all of a sudden becoming much less dangerous.[22] Erica Dyck mentions that the therapy, "…did not simply involve replacing alcohol with LSD, but instead relied on a single mega-dose

---

[22] ibid, 56

THE HISTORY OF ACID TRIPPING

(between 200 and 1,500 μg), of LSD in a

clinical environment. Patients commonly

underwent an intense reaction, followed by a

period of self-reflection that often resulted in

attitudinal changes."[23]

LSD therapy supporters found that this

route was preferable because it struck at the

heart of the problem, in that LSD could make

alcoholics reflect on the reasons that they felt

compelled to drink, as opposed to just trying

to change their behavior altogether. LSD

could quite simply make people look at the

bigger picture.[24] This is exactly the point that

Al M. Hubbard was trying to emphasize about

---

[23] ibid, 56
[24] ibid, 56

THE HISTORY OF ACID TRIPPING

alcohol recovery. Hubbard was acting in part on his own belief that an LSD trip might harbor unexplored therapeutic potential. The other driving force behind Hubbard's actions was the idea first formulated by Bill Wilson, the founder of Alcoholics Anonymous, that a religious experience was the most important factor in the recovery process for alcoholics.[25] Osmond's research with LSD and psychedelics eventually lead to alternative psychiatric theories that helped to challenge the notion that psychedelics could produce model psychoses. The authors of _Acid_

---

[25] Lee and Shlain, _Acid dreams_, 49.

THE HISTORY OF
ACID TRIPPING

Dreams: The CIA, LSD, And the Sixties

Rebellion, contend that, "…Hubbard came along and turned the young psychiatrist [Osmond] on to the religious meaning of his

THE HISTORY OF ACID TRIPPING

madness mimicking drug. The Captain [Al M. Hubbard] showed Osmond how to harness LSD's transcendental potential." If this is the case, then it may very well explain the break that Osmond had with conventional psychiatry in the 1950's in Saskatchewan.

LSD Research Takes Off in the U.S.

In October of 1955, Dr. Sydney Cohen, a psychiatrist and researcher working out of the Veterans Administration Hospital located near UCLA, tried LSD for the first time. Cohen, like many of the researchers before him, had the idea that LSD would recreate a "model psychoses" once consumed. But instead Cohen felt, "...an elevated

THE HISTORY OF ACID TRIPPING

peacefulness, as if "the problems and

strivings, the worries and frustrations of

everyday life vanished; in their place was a

majestic, sunlit, heavenly inner quietude....I

seemed to have finally arrived at the

contemplation of the eternal truth."[26] Shortly

after, Cohen would proceed to research with

LSD by measuring the effects of the drug on

81 members of the academic community.

Cohen would be disappointed with the results

of the experiment because unlike his own

experience many of the people who took part

in the experiment reported that LSD had

---

[26] Steven J. Novak, "LSD before Leary: Sidney Cohen's Critique of 1950's Psychedelic Drug Research," *Isis* Vol.88 No.1 (1997): 92, accessed November 22, 2010. http://0-www.jstor.org.torofind.csudh.edu/stable/235827.

THE HISTORY OF ACID TRIPPING

created feelings of loneliness and emptiness in them.[27] Cohen continued his research in an effort to find out if LSD could indeed be helpful in curing alcoholism, facilitating psychotherapy, and enhancing creativity. He was essentially trying to address whether or not LSD could in fact be used in a healing fashion.[28]

Cohen and his colleague, Betty Eisner, began to work in conjunction with Al M. Hubbard. Eisner and Hubbard would go on to refine methods to lessen the negative effects of LSD. Although Cohen was quite taken by these developments, he was not thoroughly

---

[27] Ibid, 92.
[28] Ibid, 95.

THE HISTORY OF ACID TRIPPING

convinced by them, Cohen would continue to prescribe to the notion that these methods were quite simply the result of suggestions being made to patients treated with LSD.[29] Despite his convictions, Cohen along with Eisner went on to report in April of 1957 a 73 percent improvement rate for twenty-two patients diagnosed for minor personality disorders that had received LSD psycho-therapy.[30] Cohen and Eisner would later go on to be present when Bill Wilson first took LSD in 1957 in Eisner's home. Steven Novak goes on to mention, "Wilson dabbled in LSD for two years, comparing its effects on occasion

---

[29] Ibid, 96.
[30] Ibid, 96.

THE HISTORY OF ACID TRIPPING

to the mystical experience at Towns Hospital

[this refers to Bill Wilson's religious

experience in 1934 when he hit rock bottom

and stopped using alcohol]. He started a

private LSD group in New York, with LSD

samples supplied by Cohen and Dr. Keith

Ditman."[31]

Dr. Sidney Cohen was a not alone in

his research on LSD; Harold Abramson also

used the drug in therapy. While working in the

South Oaks Psychiatric Hospital and Research

Foundation in Amityville, New York,

Abramson and his colleagues used LSD

psychotherapy on underage schizophrenics.

---

[31] Ibid, 97.

THE HISTORY OF ACID TRIPPING

The experiment was being recreated to compare results with Lauretta Bender, a psychiatrist also working in New York at the time who focused her efforts on studying the effects of LSD on schizophrenic and autistic children. In one experiment, Bender administered LSD to 50 children from the ages of 6 to 12 years of age with these backgrounds and published her results in 1963. She went on to conclude that some of the autistic children became happier and more responsive and affectionate when the drug was administered, while other more quiet children became mildly aggressive and unruly, even to such a point where they were biting other

THE HISTORY OF
ACID TRIPPING

children.[32] Throughout the research Abramson

kept correspondence with Drs. Sydney Cohen

and Humphrey Osmond, and the discussion

took as a larger frame of reference the effects

of LSD on children.[33] In one specific instance

Abramson and his colleagues gave LSD,

combined with three other medications, to an

11 year old suffering from severe

schizophrenia for the time period of one

month, the child was known to eat soap and

shaving cream. The study had been designed

---

[32] Lauretta Bender, G. Fratera and L. Cobrinik, "LSD and UML treatment of Hospitalized Disturbed Children," *Recent Advances in Biological Psychiatry* Vol. 5 (1963): 87, accessed November 22, 2010.
http://neurodiversity.com/library_Bender_1963.html.
[33] Harold A. Abramson, ed., *The Use of LSD in Psychotherapy and Alcoholism* (Indianapolis: Bobbs-Merrill, 1967), 622.

THE HISTORY OF ACID TRIPPING

primarily as a preliminary method for

studying LSD effects in children but also

served the purpose of being turned into a film

where different medications would be given to

the child in order to make it possible for

judges to view the film and be able to

differentiate between points in the film where

the subject was either under the influence of

LSD or another medication. The study

concludes with Harold Abramson suggesting,

"I still feel that if we do this again we'll just

use placebos and LSD, and won't try to study

whether chlorpromazine acts like LSD or not.

That's another problem and unrelated to our

THE HISTORY OF ACID TRIPPING

study".[34] The study was inconclusive thanks to the many drugs prescribed to the children prior to have been given LSD therapy.

The East Coast was also home to Timothy Leary. In the 1960's, his name would come to be synonymous with LSD. Leary stumbled onto the field of psychedelic research years after initial experimentations into LSD had begun. In his first experiment, he gave thirty-two inmates in a Massachusetts maximum security prison Psilocybin, the active ingredient in mushrooms that produce hallucinations, in an effort to find out if the drug would change the prisoners and in the

---

[34] Ibid, 625.

THE HISTORY OF ACID TRIPPING

process bring down their recidivism rate.[35] In

his experiments, at least one member of

Leary's researchers would take the drug with

the prisoners while others observed. The study

concluded on the high note that only 25

percent of the prisoners that took the drug

returned to prison, the normal rate being 80.[36]

---

[35] Lee and Shlain, *Acid dreams*, 75.
[36] Ibid, 75

THE HISTORY OF ACID TRIPPING

Leary later went on, with the help of a PhD candidate, to give the drug to a control group of ten theology students and professors. The results of this experiment showed that nine of the ten participants in the control group given psilocybin reported to have had a deeply religious experience, as opposed to only member of the control-group given placebos instead.[37] Leary would later run into trouble with the administration at Harvard for distributing psilocybin outside experiments and for not having a medical doctor present when he administered the psychedelic agents.

---

[37] Ibid, 76

THE HISTORY OF ACID TRIPPING

LSD research in the United States picked up quite quickly and the experiments would not be limited to humans. In 1962, Dr. Louis Jolyon West and his staff at the University of Oklahoma decided to try and artificially reproduce the period in a male elephants' life known as musth. During this period the animal secretes a brown sticky fluid from a gland halfway between the animal's eye and ear. Elephants are also known to grow overly restless and aggressive. West was prescribing to the notion that LSD could still be used to recreate "madness", and so West decided to do so he mentions in <u>Science</u> magazine, "Recently we decide to induce

THE HISTORY OF ACID TRIPPING

experimentally a behavioral aberration that
might resemble the phenomenon of going on
musth. The animal involved was Tusko
(estimated age, 14 years), a male Indian
elephant (Elephas maximus indicus) that was
being boarded at the Lincoln Park Zoo in
Oklahoma City. D-Lysergic acid diethylamide
(LSD) was chosen as the psychotomimetic
agent because of its well known personality-
disrupting effect upon humans and other
animals. Should Tusko's reaction to an
injection of LSD resemble going on musth, we
wanted to see whether there would occur
simultaneously an excretion of the

THE HISTORY OF ACID TRIPPING

DRAFT
9 June 1953

MEMORANDUM FOR THE RECORD

SUBJECT: Project MKULTRA, Subproject 8

   1. Subproject 8 is being set up as a means to continue the present work in the general field of L.S.D. at until 11 September 1954.

   2. This project will include a continuation of a study of the biochemical, neurophysiological, sociological, and clinical psychiatric aspects of L.S.D., and also a study of L.S.D. antagonists and drugs related to L.S.D., such as L.A.E. A detailed proposal is attached. The principle investigators will continue to be all of

   3. The estimated budget of the project at is $39,500.00. The will serve as a cut-out and cover for this project and will furnish the above funds to the as a philanthropic grant for medical research. A service charge of $750.00 (2% of the estimated budget) is to be paid to the for this service.

   4. Thus the total charges for this project will not exceed $40,290.00 for a period ending September 11, 1954.

   5. (Director of the hospital) are cleared through TOP SECRET and are aware of the true purpose of the project.

Chemical Division/TSS

APPROVED:

Chief, Chemical Division/TSS

PROGRAM

temporal glands and, if possible, to collect

some of the fluid".[38] The elephant was given a

---

[38] Louis Jolyon West, Chester M. Pierce and Warren D. Thomas, "Lysergic Acid Diethylamide: Its Effects on a

THE HISTORY OF ACID TRIPPING

total of 300,000 micrograms, and the authors

of _Acid Dreams_ contend that West was a CIA

contract employee and a firm believer in the

notion that hallucinogens were

psychotomimetic [madness inducing]

agents.[39] Tusko was injected with LSD and

soon became restless, his mate [Judy, a 15

year old female] then tried to console him but

it was to no avail, Tusko collapsed on his right

side, defecated, and then hyper-extended his

muscles and he began to have trouble

breathing; at the site of this he was given an

injection of promazine hydrochloride and

Male Asiatic Elephant," _Science_ Vol.138 No.3545 (1962):
1101, accessed November 22, 2010. http://0-
www.jstor.org.torofind.csudh.edu/stable/1709491
[39] Lee and Shlain, _Acid Dreams_, 22.

THE HISTORY OF ACID TRIPPING

another of pentobarbital sodium but he died

anyway an hour and forty minutes after the

last injection.[40]

LSD: The CIA and the Army

LSD came to the doorsteps of the CIA

in 1951. The drug first came to the attention of

the agency in response to the search for a drug

that could serve either the purpose of mind

control or as a truth serum. In his book, _The_

Search for the Manchurian Candidate, John

Marks mentions that, "Sydney Gottlieb [an

LSD researcher working for the CIA's TSS

unit, Technical Services Staff was the CIA

unit in charge of the MK-ULTRA program

---

[40] West, Pierce, and Thomas, "Lysergic Acid Elephant,"
1101.

THE HISTORY OF ACID TRIPPING

that conducted experiments with LSD] later

testified that the purpose of these programs

was 'to investigate whether and how it was

possible to modify and individual's behavior

by covert means'.[41] Dr. Sid Gottlieb, with

CIA aid, later began funding LSD research.

The agency funded the research through the

Geschickter Fund for Medical Research and

the Josiah Macy, Jr. Foundation. Those

involved in the research included; Harold

Abramson, Louis Jolyon West, Carl Pfeiffer,

and Harris Isbell who worked out of the

Addiction Research Center in Kentucky.[42]

---

[41] John Marks, *The Search for the Manchurian Candidate*
(New York: McGraw-Hill, 1980), 57.
[42] Ibid , 59

THE HISTORY OF ACID TRIPPING

The drug was tested in preliminary trials on a military officer and showed promise as an amnesia inducing agent, since military intelligence had successfully been extracted from the officer in an experiment with the drug and he had no recollection of what had happened.[43] The use of LSD would later be altered. This was so because the drug could cause extreme anxiety in an interrogation process or could lead a subject to believe that he could defy his interrogators. LSD's lack of odor, color, and taste made it appealing to the spy trade. LSD would eventually evolve within the CIA into an anti-interrogation drug

---

[43] Lee and Shlain, *Acid dreams*, 14.

THE HISTORY OF ACID TRIPPING

the authors of _Acid Dreams_ mention, "since

information obtained from a person in a

psychotic state would be unrealistic, bizarre,

and extremely difficult to assess, the self-

administration of LSD-25, which is effective

in minute doses, might in special

circumstances offer an operative temporary

protection against interrogation."[44] The

agency believed that the Russians and the

Chinese could be making use of the drug,

since ergot was a commercial product in

Eastern Bloc countries.[45]

Shortly after 1951, the CIA began to

give LSD to agents in case they were captured

---

[44] ibid, 16
[45] ibid, 16

and interrogated while on the field. The

agency also planned to give LSD to CIA

trainee volunteers to determine which subjects

(+)-LSD
configuration: (5R,8R)

(−)-LSD
configuration: (5S,8S)

Base

Base

(+)-iso-LSD
configuration: (5R,8S)

(−)-iso-LSD
configuration: (5S,8R)

would react with extreme anxiety to the drug

in order to exclude those subjects from more

critical assignments.[46] The CIA refined its use

of LSD in interrogations and used the drug in

---

[46] ibid, 17

THE HISTORY OF ACID TRIPPING

operations from the 1950's through the early

1960's. CIA agents capitalized on the intense

mental confusion brought about in subjects by

LSD, and interrogators would threaten

subjects with indefinitely extending the effects

of LSD unless the subject agreed to talk.[47]

In 1953, the CIA bought LSD from the

Sandoz Corporation and, in the process,

managed to convince the corporation to

provide the agency with a list of customers

purchasing LSD. John Marks writes, "He [the

Sandoz Corporation president] also agreed to

pass any intelligence about Eastern European

interest in LSD. The Sandoz executives asked

---

[47] ibid, 19

THE HISTORY OF ACID TRIPPING

only that their arrangement with the CIA be

kept 'in the very strictest of confidence.'[48]

The agency also asked Eli-Lilly & Company

to synthesize the drug so as to not have to rely

on a foreign entity for LSD. By mid 1954 the

company had succeeded in producing the first

batch of LSD in the United States, this first

batch was donated to the U.S. government.[49]

In 1954, agents within the CIA first took LSD

in pairs and reported their experiences to each

other in an effort to become more familiar

with the inebriation caused by the drug. The

agency then proceeded to do as the authors of

Acid Dreams mention, "...they agreed among

---

[48] Marks, *The Search for the Manchurian*, 66.
[49] ibid, 66-67

THE HISTORY OF ACID TRIPPING

themselves to slip LSD into each other's

drinks. The target never knew when his turn

would come, but as soon as the drug was

ingested a TSS colleague would tell him so he

could make the necessary preparations-which

usually meant taking the rest of the day off".[50]

The objective behind the dosing had been to

try and figure out how the CIA could use LSD

in the spy trade.

Soon enough other agency personnel

were being dosed and a plan by the TSS to

spike the punch at the annual Christmas office

party was foiled.[51] In November of 1953, CIA

and Army personnel gathered for a work

---

[50] Lee and Shlain, *Acid Dreams*, 29.
[51] ibid 29

THE HISTORY OF ACID TRIPPING

retreat, LSD was laced into cocktails. John Marks maintains that, "Unbeknownst to the SOD [Army Chemical Corp's Special Operations Division, of which Frank Olson was part of] men, Sid Gottlieb had decided to spike the liqueur with LSD."[52] Dr. Frank Olson, who was a biological warfare researcher with the Army, was among those dosed; he slipped into depression shortly afterwards and was sent to see Harold Abramson in New York after his behavior continued to be erratic. Abramson concluded that Olson was delusional and psychotic. His last night in New York Olson fell 10 stories

---

[52] Marks, *The search for the Manchurian*, 77.

from his hotel window and died.[53] His death

would later be attributed by some to the CIA.

The CIA went on to test LSD on

unsuspecting subjects by having prostitutes

slip the drug to their clients and having agency

personnel watch the ordeals in a safe house

located in New York's Greenwich Village

retrofitted with surveillance equipment and

two way mirrors.[54] The authors of *Acid*

Dreams go on to say that, "CIA documents

cited in a documentary by the ABC News

confirm that Gottlieb carried a stash of acid

[LSD] overseas on a number of occasions

during the Cold War with the intention of

---

[53]Lee and Shlain, *Acid Dreams*, 31.
[54] ibid 32

THE HISTORY OF ACID TRIPPING

dosing foreign diplomats and statesmen."[55]

As early as 1953, Gottlieb had been carrying hallucinogens overseas; he even covertly slipped LSD to a public speaker in an effort to see if the drug would cause the speaker to embarrass himself.[56]

The Army had plans to use LSD as a "madness gas" to incapacitate people as a means to avoid warfare casualties.[57] In the late 1950's the Army tested LSD on soldiers at Fort Bragg, North Carolina, to see how well soldiers performed war games while on the drug. The results showed that psychedelic

---

[55] ibid 35
[56] Marks, *The Search for the Manchurian*, 68.
[57] Lee and Shlain, *Acid Dreams*, 36.

THE HISTORY OF ACID TRIPPING

agents could be used to incapacitate soldiers.

The Army Chemical Corps decided that in

order to avoid a scenario where LSD could be

used covertly against a military unit, every

officer should be acquainted with the drug.

The authors of _Acid Dreams_ write,

"Accordingly nearly two hundred officers

assigned to the Chemical Corps School at Fort

McClellan, Alabama, were given acid as a

supplement to their regular training program.

Some staff members even tried to teach

classes while tripping."[58]Needless to say the

subjects within the Army receiving LSD were

not exactly having a good time. The Army

---

[58] ibid, 39

THE HISTORY OF ACID TRIPPING

gave soldiers at Edgewood Arsenal LSD and
then confined them to sensory deprivation
chambers in an effort to ready soldiers for the
event of an interrogation by an enemy. The
Army also deprived the soldiers of human
contact, food, work, sleep, and even bodily
evacuation in these experiments.[59] By the mid
1960's, almost 1500 soldiers were
experimented on with LSD, and the drug was
stolen by soldiers from Army labs for
recreational use. The Army soon abandoned
their experiments on LSD because of the
development of BZ, better known as nerve
gas.

---

[59] ibid, 39

THE HISTORY OF ACID TRIPPING

Popularizing LSD: Psychiatry and Leary

Revisited

The psychiatric community of the 1950's and 1960's was heavily invested in the diffusion of LSD into mainstream American society. Dr, Sydney Cohen was among those psychiatrists that aided LSD's diffusion by introducing the drug to the artistic community in an effort to find subjects that could verbalize their experiences. Such was the case when Humphrey Osmond first gave mescaline to Aldous Huxley and when Sydney Cohen later did the same in collaboration with Huxley and his friend Gerald Heard. Steven J. Novak tells us, "that physicians like Osmond

THE HISTORY OF ACID TRIPPING

and Cohen would turn to nonmedical thinkers like Huxley and Heard was partly due to psychiatry's lack of an adequate model of mental illness, such as the germ theory provided for infectious disease."[60] The author goes on to mention that it was Huxley that redefined the taking of mescaline and LSD into a religious experience. Soon Huxley managed to get Humphrey Osmond and Albert Hoffmann to accept this religious idea.[61]

This religious viewpoint would later come to be adopted and expanded on by Timothy Leary. In an interview for Playboy

---

[60] Novak, "LSD before Leary," 95.
[61] Ibid, 93-94

THE HISTORY OF ACID TRIPPING

magazine in 1966, Leary mentions that LSD

and psychedelic drugs were very readily

accepted by people under the age of twenty

five. In the article Leary says, "...that sexual

ecstasy [as experienced through sex while on

LSD] is the basic reason for the current LSD

boom."[62] Leary contends that he moved away

from the conventional places for

administering LSD, the laboratory or the

hospital in favor of more familiar settings for

subjects like their homes, because he shared

Albert Hoffmann's notion that therapists

---

[62] Bernard Gavzer, "Playboy Interview: Timothy Leary a candid conversation with the controversial ex-harvard professor, prime partisan and prophet of LSD," *Playboy Magazine*, Sep. 1966, accessed November 22, 2010. http://www.archive.org/details/playboylearyinte00playric h. pg. 4.

THE HISTORY OF ACID TRIPPING

should take LSD with their patients or at least

have some experience with the drug in order

to act as an effective guide for their patients

through an LSD session.[63] In reference to the

proper setting for an LSD session, Leary goes

on to add, "Take LSD in a nuthouse and you'll

have a nuthouse experience."[64] To Leary, the

psychiatric professionals were simply not

prepared to effectively take a subject through

an LSD session. Leary's group was looked

down upon by the scientific community, but it

didn't matter to Leary because his subjects

had positive experiences with LSD, versus

those who had taken the drug in a laboratory

---

[63] Ibid, 9
[64] Ibid, 9

THE HISTORY OF ACID TRIPPING

setting; Leary claimed that 99 percent of the people he administered LSD had an enjoyable experience.

When it came to the use of LSD, Leary became a universalist in that he believed that LSD and the exploration of consciousness should be available to everyone. He even went as far as to suggest that there should be a test, similar to a drivers' license test, so that people could responsibly use LSD. Leary felt that 15 year olds had the appropriate level of "energy" to make use of LSD. He held LSD to be a "cure" for homosexuality and even offered up the example of Allen Ginsberg, who first opened up to the opposite sex at an

THE HISTORY OF ACID TRIPPING

LSD session.[65] But in the end Leary also mentions that, "LSD is no guarantee of any specific social or sexual outcome." [66]

The popularization of LSD by multiple psychiatrist proved to be a great point of diffusion for LSD into the general populace. Steven J. Novak mentions of Harold Abramson, "On Long Island, Abramson began holding Friday-night LSD soirees in his home and was besieged by people who wanted to take the drug. In 1965 Abramson said, 'It was all I could do to prevent all of Brookhaven, people in the school system, friends, and so

---

[65] Ibid, 5
[66] Ibid, 5

THE HISTORY OF ACID TRIPPING

on, to come to dinner with us on Friday evenings to take LSD.'[67]

Ken Kesey and the Merry Pranksters: A Less Serious Approach to LSD

The Merry Pranksters were put together by Ken Kesey the author of *One Flew Over the Cuckoo's Nest*. The group would go on to travel around the country during the 1960's, by first venturing out in 1964 to Phoenix, Arizona. The goal of the group was to go around and turn people on to the expansion of consciousness using LSD and other drugs like speed and marijuana. Ken Kesey had been arrested on two charges for

---

[67] Novak, "LSD before Leary," 99.

THE HISTORY OF ACID TRIPPING

possession of marijuana and had spent some

time down in Mexico exploring the use of

hallucinogenic drugs, but now he was ready to

change the way people viewed psychedelic

drugs and he planned to do so by starting a

movement to take the LSD experience

throughout the country.[68]

In hoping for some comprehension, the

Merry Pranksters decided to take their group

up to New York so that they could meet up

with Leary and his camp in the Millbrook

---

[68] Tom Wolfe, *The Electric Kool-Aid Acid Test* (New York: Farrar Straus And Giroux, 1968), 6 and 10-11.

THE HISTORY OF ACID TRIPPING

estate. The meeting of the two groups seemed

almost logical. Both Ken Kesey and Timothy

Leary had been to Mexico to experiment with

psychedelic drugs, and most of all they both

THE HISTORY OF ACID TRIPPING

propagated the message that LSD should be

universally available to everyone. Instead,

upon arrival the Merry Pranksters were

greeted by a small reception representing the

Leary camp. The group told Kesey and the

Merry Pranksters that Timothy Leary would

not personally be receiving the group since he

was experimenting on a three day trip in the

upper portion of the mansion located on the

Millbrook estate. Author Tom Wolfe writes of

the event in his book, The Electric Kool-Aid

Acid Test, "[Ken] Kesey wasn't angry, but he

was very disappointed, even hurt."[69] Authors

Martin A. Lee and Bruce Shlain write of the

---

[69] Ibid, 108

THE HISTORY OF ACID TRIPPING

Leary/Pranksters encounter, "The Millbrook

group was essentially made up of behavioral

scientists who kept records of their mental

states, wrote papers and put out a journal.

Leary and his people were going the

scholarly route, giving lectures and such; they

had nothing to gain by associating with a

THE HISTORY OF ACID TRIPPING

bunch of grinning, filthy bums wearing

buckskins and face paint. The distance

between the East Coast intellectuals and

Kesey's clan was cavernous. As

Michael Hollingshead [the owner of the

Millbrook estate] recalled, 'They thought we

were square and we thought they were

crazy'.[70]

The story would be completely

different when Ken Kesey invited 40 Hell's

Angels to his home in La Honda, California.

The Hell's Angels and the Merry Pranksters

hit it off right away. The police did nothing to

intervene, they simply contained the event.

---

[70] Lee and Shlain, *Acid dreams*, 124.

THE HISTORY OF ACID TRIPPING

The event went through without a hitch and the Angels never had to fight. Beer and LSD flowed without end and observers described the Hell's Angels on LSD as peaceful. The party raged on for two days and Allen Ginsberg even pranced around a microphone singing Hare Krishna with finger cymbals.[71] Through their efforts the Merry Pranksters were able to bring LSD to the masses, and the break with the Leary camp only helped them to spread the message into the farthest subgroups of society, as was the case with the Hell's Angels.

---

[71] Wolfe, *The Electric Kool-Aid*, 174.

THE HISTORY OF ACID TRIPPING

LSD; Musicians and Artists

Poet Allen Ginsberg first tried LSD at the Mental Research Institute in Palo Alto, California. Ginsberg had a particularly hard time with his first LSD trip in part because of the clinical setting. He had the staff hook up a flicker machine to an EGG apparatus so that he could see the rhythm of the alpha waves in his brain in conjunction with the flickering light. Ginsberg mentions, "It was like watching my own inner organism."[72] To Ginsberg, the experience was overwhelming. Arithmetic problems and Rorschach inkblots were part of the experiment, and to the poet

---

[72] Lee and Shlain, *Acid dreams*, 56-57.

THE HISTORY OF ACID TRIPPING

such things were trivial in the peak of an LSD

trip. Ginsberg would soon start taking LSD

with Timothy Leary, but when the religious

experiences that Leary preached never came,

he began to feel that enlightenment was out of

his reach and developed a compulsive need to

take LSD.[73] In his process of psychedelic

exploration, Ginsberg managed to introduce

the jazz musicians Theolonius Monk and

Dizzy Gillespie to psilocybin and other

psychedelics.[74] The bad trips soon became too

common for Ginsberg, and it was not until he

tossed out Leary's religious interpretations of

---

[73] Ibid, 111
[74] Ibid ,79

THE HISTORY OF
ACID TRIPPING

LSD that he could begin to actually enjoy his

experiences on the drug. [75]

The Beatles had LSD slipped into their

coffee by a dentist the first time they tripped,

George Harrison mentions that, at the time,

LSD was an unrestricted medication. John

Lennon stopped taking the drug because he

had too many bad trips, but he didn't develop

a bias against the use of the drug. George

Harrison seemed to have the act of taking

LSD down to an art, his experiences tended to

be positive, because he didn't let the drug take

control of him and his thought process.

George also felt more closely connected to

---

[75] Ibid, 112-113

THE HISTORY OF ACID TRIPPING

PROJECT MKULTRA, THE CIA'S PROGRAM OF
RESEARCH IN BEHAVIORAL MODIFICATION

JOINT HEARING
BEFORE THE
SELECT COMMITTEE ON INTELLIGENCE
AND THE
SUBCOMMITTEE ON
HEALTH AND SCIENTIFIC RESEARCH
OF THE
COMMITTEE ON HUMAN RESOURCES
UNITED STATES SENATE
NINETY-FIFTH CONGRESS
FIRST SESSION

AUGUST 3, 1977

Printed for the use of the Select Committee on Intelligence
and Committee on Human Resources

U.S. GOVERNMENT PRINTING OFFICE
95-408 O   WASHINGTON : 1977
For sale by the Superintendent of Documents, U.S. Government Printing Office
Washington, D.C. 20402
Stock No. 052-070-04357-1

John Lennon because of their acid trips. This

is the reason they decided to give LSD to Paul

McCartney and Ringo Starr in Los Angeles.

THE HISTORY OF ACID TRIPPING

George mentions, "That is another thing; when two people take it at the same time; words become redundant. One can see what the other is thinking. You look at each other and know".[76] George, ironically, had his break with drugs when he visited the Haight-Ashbury and people were doing STP, a super hallucinogen that is similar to LSD but its effects last 3 days.[77] John Lennon mentions, "We must always remember to thank the CIA and the Army for LSD, by the way…They brought out LSD to control people, and what they did was give us freedom."[78] John wrote

---

[76] The Beatles, *The Beatles Anthology* (Hong Kong: Apple Corps Ltd, 2000), 180.
[77] Ibid 259
[78] Ibid, 179

THE HISTORY OF ACID TRIPPING

the song "She said, she said" in reference to

the time the Beatles took LSD in L.A. with

Peter Fonda and he kept telling John, "I know

what it is like to be dead".[79] Jimi Hendrix,

much like the Beatles, took LSD for the first

time without knowing what it was. Charles R.

Gross mentions in his book, _Room Full of_

Mirrors, "Jimi was asked if he'd be interested

in taking some acid. His answer showed both

his naïveté and his complete inexperience with

psychedelics. 'No, I don't want none of that',

he said, 'but I'd love to try some of that LSD

stuff.'[80] And like the Beatles, the drug was

---

[79] Ibid, 190
[80]Charles R. Gross, _Room Full of Mirrors: A Biography of Jimi Hendrix_ (New York: Hyperion, 2005), 132.

THE HISTORY OF ACID TRIPPING

still legal when Hendrix decided to take it.

Hendrix used LSD as an escape from being himself, as well as to help him write songs, but he was careful about not sounding like an advocate of the drug in front of the media. The song "Purple Haze" referred to a stash of LSD that he would keep in a bullet; this was also due to the fact that the drug was purple.

Charles R. Gross goes on to mention that, at the Monterey Pop Festival, "Jimi timed his own acid trip so that his peak would come during the middle of his set".[81] LSD would later become a pillar that Hendrix relied on in order to perfect his music.

---

[81] Ibid, 193

THE HISTORY OF ACID TRIPPING

Conclusion

The story of LSD came to an abrupt end in the spring of 1966 when the drug was declared illegal. President Nixon launched a war on drugs that would come to define government policy towards psychedelics and drugs in general. In the Senate hearings of 1966 Allen Ginsberg tried to show that a large part of the negative light surrounding LSD use was a construct of the media demonizing LSD.[82] In the end he was unsuccessful and the opportunity for legitimate research to be conducted on LSD was lost as well. The topics covered in this paper lead me to

---

[82] Lee and Shlain, *Acid Dreams*, 153.

THE HISTORY OF ACID TRIPPING

conclude that there was no one reason why the counter-culture of the 1960's so readily accepted psychedelic drugs. Rather psychedelic drugs had long been on everybody's minds. The CIA, the Army, and the psychiatric community were only a few of the many factions interested in the psychoactive properties of LSD. Why psychedelic drugs didn't pierce society any sooner is simply matter of diffusion. It took time for the word of LSD to reach mainstream society but once it did society as Americans had known it changed forever.

THE HISTORY OF ACID TRIPPING

Bibliography

Beatles, The. *The Beatles Anthology*. Hong Kong: Apple Corps Ltd, 2000.

Bender, Lauretta. "LSD and UML treatment of Hospitalized Disturbed Children." *Recent Advances in Biological Psychiatry Vol. 5* (1963): 84-92. Accessed November 22, 2010. http://neurodiversity.com/library_Bender_196 3.html.

Dyck, Ericka. "The Land of the Living Sky with Diamonds: A place for Radical Psychiatry." *Journal of Canadian Stuides* (2007): 42-66. Accessed, November 22, 2010. http://0muse.jhu.edu.torofind.csudh.edu/searc h/results?search_id=2055295640&action=relo ad.

Bernard Gavzer. "Playboy Interview: Timothy Leary a candid conversation with the controversial ex-harvard professor, prime partisan and prophet of LSD." *Playboy Magazine*, Sep. (1966): 2-14. Accessed November 22, 2010. HYPERLINK "http://www.archive.org/details/playboylearyi nte00playrich"

THE HISTORY OF ACID TRIPPING

http://www.archive.org/details/playboylearyin
te00playrich .

Gross, Charles R. *Room Full of Mirrors: A Biography of Jimi Hendrix* . New York: Hyperion, 2005.

Harold A. Abramson, editor. *The Use of LSD in Psychotherapy and Alcoholism.* Indianapolis: Bobbs-Merrill , 1967.

Hoffmann, Albert. *LSD: My Problem Child.* New York: McGraw-Hill, 1980.

Louis Jolyon West, Chester M. Pierce and Warren D. Thomas. "Lysergic Acid Diethylamide: Its Effects on a Male Asiatic Elephant." *Science* (1962): 1100-1103. Accessed November 22, 2010. http://0-www.jstor.org.torofind.csudh.edu/stable/1709491

Marks, John. *The Search for the Manchurian Candidate* . New York: McGraw-Hill, 1980.

Novak, Steven J. "LSD before Leary: Sidney Cohen's Critique of 1950's Psychedelic Drug Research." *Isis* (1997): 87-110. Accessed November 22, 2010. http://0-

THE HISTORY OF ACID TRIPPING

www.jstor.org.torofind.csudh.edu/stable/2358 27.

Saldanha, Arun. "The LSD Event: Badiou Not on Acid." *Theory and Event Vol. 10, No. 4* (2007): 1-58. Accesed November 22, 2010. http://0-muse.jhu.edu.torofind.csudh.edu/journals/theo ry_and_event/v010/10.4saldanha.html.

Shlain, Martin A. Lee and Bruce. *Acid Dreams: the CIA, LSD and the Sixties Rebellion*. New York: Grove Press, 1985.

Wolfe, Tom. *The Electric Kool-Aid Acid Test*. New York : Farrar Straus And Giroux, 1968.

Appendix A

Delysid (LSD 25) *D-lysergic acid*

diethylamide tartrate

PROPERTIES
The administration of very small doses of Delysid (½-2 μg./kg. body weight) results in transitory
disturbances of affect, hallucinations, depersonalization, reliving of repressed memories, and mild neuro-vegetative

THE HISTORY OF ACID TRIPPING

symptoms. The effect sets in after 30 to 90 minutes and generally lasts 5 to 12 hours. However, intermittent disturbances of affect may occasionally persist for several days.

INDICATIONS AND DOSAGE

a) Analytical psychotherapy, to elicit release of repressed material and provide mental relaxation, particularly in anxiety states and obsessional neuroses. The initial dose is 25 μg. (¼ of an ampoule or 1 tablet). This dose is increased at each treatment by 25 μg. until the optimum dose (usually between 50 and 200 μg.) is found. The individual treatments are best given at intervals of one week.

b) Experimental studies on the nature of psychoses: By taking Delysid himself, the psychiatrist is able to gain an insight in the world of ideas and sensations of mental patients. Delysid can also be used to induce model psychoses of short duration in normal subjects, this facilitates studies on the pathogenesis of mental disease.

In normal subjects, doses of 25 to 75 μg. are generally sufficient to produce a hallucinatory psychosis (on an average 1 μg./kg. body weight). In certain forms of psychosis and in

THE HISTORY OF ACID TRIPPING

chronic alcoholism, higher doses are necessary (2 to 4 μg./kg. body weight).

PRECAUTIONS

Pathological mental conditions may be intensified by Delysid. Particular caution is necessary in subjects with a suicidal tendency and in those cases where a psychotic development appears imminent. The psycho-affective liability and the tendency to commit impulsive acts may occasionally last for some days.

Delysid should only be administered under strict medical supervision. The supervision should not be discontinued until the effects of the drug have completely worn off.

ANTIDOTE

The mental effects of Delysid can be rapidly reversed by the i.m. administration of 50 mg. chlorpromazine

THE HISTORY OF ACID TRIPPING

INTERESTING FACTS!

- In 2001, almost 1.4 million youths aged 12 to 17 had used hallucinogens at least once in their lifetime.

- Among youths, blacks were less likely than whites, Asians, or Hispanics to have used any hallucinogen in their lifetime.

- Blacks and Hispanics were more likely than whites and Asians to perceive great risk in trying LSD once or twice.

Source: NHSDA & US DOJ

THE HISTORY OF ACID TRIPPING

Street Terms for LSD

Back breaker

Battery acid

Blot

Doses

Dots

Elvis

Hits

Loony toons

Lucy in the sky with diamonds

Pane

Superman

Tabs

Window pane

Zen

THE HISTORY OF ACID TRIPPING

Glossary (Mini)

Acid: Common street name for LSD.

Angel dust: Common street name for PCP.

Bad Trip: Refers to a negative experience by an LSD user while on the substance.

Cerebral cortex: Region of the brain responsible for cognitive functions including reasoning, mood, and perception of stimuli.

Dissociative anesthetic: Compound, such as phencyclidine or ketamine, that produces an anesthetic effect characterized by a feeling of being detached from the physical self.

THE HISTORY OF ACID TRIPPING

DXM: Common street name for dextromethorphan.

Flashback: Slang term for HPPD (see below).

Glutamate: A neurotransmitter associated with pain, memory, and response to changes in the environment.

Hallucinogen: A drug that produces hallucinations - distortion in perception of sights and sounds - and disturbances in emotion, judgment, and memory.

HPPD: Hallucinogen persisting perception disorder; the spontaneous and sometimes continuous recurrence of perceptual effects of LSD long after an individual has ingested the drug.

THE HISTORY OF ACID TRIPPING

Ketamine: Dissociative anesthetic abused for its mind-altering effects and sometimes used to facilitate sexual assault.

Locus ceruleus: Region of the brain that receives and processes sensory signals from all areas of the body.

Neurotransmitter: Chemical compound that acts as a messenger to carry signals or stimuli from one nerve cell to another.

NMDA: *N*-methyl-D-aspartate, a chemical compound that reacts with glutamate receptors on nerve cells.

PCP: Phencyclidine, a dissociative anesthetic abused for its mind-altering effects.

THE HISTORY OF ACID TRIPPING

Persistent psychosis: Unpredictable and long-lasting visual disturbances, dramatic mood swings, and hallucinations experienced by some LSD users after they have discontinued use of the drug.

Serotonin: A neurotransmitter that causes a very broad range of effects on perception, movement, and the emotions by modulating the actions of other neurotransmitters in most parts of the brain.

THE HISTORY OF ACID TRIPPING

D-LYSERGIC ACID DIETHYLAMIDE
(Street Names: LSD, Acid, Blotter Acid, Window Pane)

December 2010
DEA/OD/ODE

Introduction:

Lysergic acid diethylamide (LSD), commonly referred to as "acid", is a synthetic hallucinogen. LSD is very potent, only microgram amounts are required to produce overt hallucinations. LSD has been abused since the 1960s. LSD's availability has declined significantly since 2001.

Licit Uses:

There is no legitimate medical use for LSD in the United States.

Chemistry and Pharmacology:

LSD is manufactured from lysergic acid, which is found in ergot, a fungus that grows on rye and other grains. LSD's physiological effects are mediated primarily through the serotonergic neuronal system.

THE HISTORY OF ACID TRIPPING

LSD induces a heightened awareness of sensory input that is accompanied by an enhanced sense of clarity, but reduced ability to control what is experienced. The LSD trip is made up of perceptual and psychic effects. A user may experience the following perceptual effects: visual distortion in the size and shape of objects, movements, color, sound, touch, and the user's own body image. The user may report "hearing colors" or "seeing sounds." The psychic effects experienced by the user may include a feelings of obtaining true insight, intensified emotions, sudden and dramatic mood swings, impairment of attention, concentration and motivation, distortion of time, and depersonalization.

The adverse effects experienced with LSD use are dependent on the dose taken by the users. Some of the adverse effects reported are dilated pupils, raised body temperature, increased heart rate and blood pressure, profuse sweating, loss of appetite, sleeplessness, dry mouth and tremors.

High doses of LSD can induce a "bad trip" characterized by intense anxiety or panic, confusion, and combative behaviors. After a LSD trip, a user may also experience fatigue,

THE HISTORY OF ACID TRIPPING

acute anxiety, or depression for 12 to 24 hours.

Illicit Uses:

LSD is abused for its hallucinogenic effects. LSD is sold in a variety of forms, tablets, capsules, and liquid. The average effective oral dose is from 20 to 80 micrograms. Following ingestion, effects occur within 30 to 60 minutes and last 10 to 12 hours.

The 2009 Monitoring the Future (MTF) report indicated that the annual prevalence of LSD use among students in 8th, 10th, and 12th grades was 1.1%, 1.9% and 1.9%, respectively. The annual prevalence of 12th grade use of LSD decreased significantly from 2.7% in 2008 to 1.9% in 2009. According to the American Association of Poison Control Centers, 357 case mentions and 204 single exposures related to LSD were reported to the National Poison Data System in 2008. The 2009 National Survey on Drug Use and Health (NSDUH) indicated that 23.6 million people in the U.S. population, aged 12 and older, used LSD in their lifetime. In 2009 alone, 779,000 of them used LSD. The Drug Abuse Warning Network (DAWN ED) reports that an estimated 4,002 emergency department

THE HISTORY OF ACID TRIPPING

visits were associated with LSD in 2006, 3,561 visits in 2007 and 3,287 visits in 2008.

User Population:

LSD is abused by teenagers and young adults in connection with "raves," nightclubs, and concert settings.

Illicit Distribution:

According the DEA System to Retrieve Information from Drug Evidence (STRIDE), the number of LSD items seized decreased dramatically in 2002 due to the seizure of a large LSD lab in Kansas City in 2000. With the arrest of clandestine chemists and with the dismantling of their laboratory, the availability of LSD in the U.S. was reduced by 95% within 2 years. In subsequent years, seizures of LSD increased, and most recently, seizures have once again decreased.

According to the National Forensic Laboratory Information System (NFLIS) and the System to Retrieve Information from Drug Evidence (STRIDE), law enforcement officials submitted 1,229 and 984 LSD exhibits to federal, state and local forensic laboratories in 2008 and 2009, respectively.

THE HISTORY OF ACID TRIPPING

From January to September 2010, law enforcement officials submitted 748 LSD exhibits to forensic laboratories.

LSD is odorless, colorless and tasteless. It is sold in a variety of formulations. Some of the streets names include acid, battery acid, blotter, window pane, microdots, Loony toons, Sunshine, and Zen. Prices range from $2 to $5 per unit or "hit."

LSD is most commonly found in the form of small squares of paper called blotter; that is generally decorated with artwork or designs, perforated, soaked in liquid LSD solution, and dried. Each square represents one dose of LSD. There have been some instances of blotter paper being found impregnated with hallucinogens other than LSD. The hallucinogens, 2,5-dimethoxyamphetamine (DMA), 4-bromo-2,5-dimethoxyamphetamine (DOB), 4-iodo-2,5-dimethoxyphenethylamine (2C-I), and 4-iodo-2,5-dimethoxyamphetamine (DOI) have been found on blotter paper passed off as LSD.

Other forms of LSD include tablets (known as microdots), gelatin squares (known as window pane), and impregnated sugar cubes. LSD has also been available in gel wraps which look

THE HISTORY OF ACID TRIPPING

like "bubble-wrap" packing material, and is blue in color. LSD is also distributed in liquid form which often is packaged in small bottles typically sold as breath drops. Additionally, LSD has been embedded in candy such as "Gummy Worms," "Sweet Tarts," "Smartie," and "Pez." The most common venues for retail LSD distribution are "raves," dance clubs, and concerts.

Control Status:

Lysergic acid diethylamide acid is in schedule I of the Controlled Substances Act (CSA). Its two precursor's lysergic acid and lysergic acid amide are both in schedule III of the CSA. The LSD precursors, ergotamine and ergonovine, are List I chemicals.

Source:
http://www.deadiversion.usdoj.gov/drugs_concern/lsd/lsd.htm

THE HISTORY OF ACID TRIPPING

INDEX

THE HISTORY OF ACID TRIPPING

ACKNOWLEDGEMENTS

CSU Dominguez Hills

Kambiz Mostofizadeh

Mikazuki Publishing

My friends and Family

Bookstore Owners

Ingram Books

THE HISTORY OF
ACID TRIPPING
NOTES
(Please use this page for comments)

THE HISTORY OF ACID TRIPPING

NOTES

(Please use this page for comments)

THE HISTORY OF ACID TRIPPING

NOTES

(Please use this page for comments)

THE HISTORY OF ACID TRIPPING

NOTES

(Please use this page for comments)

THE HISTORY OF
ACID TRIPPING

NOTES
(Please use this page for comments)

THE HISTORY OF ACID TRIPPING

NOTES

(Please use this page for comments)

THE HISTORY OF ACID TRIPPING

NOTES
(Please use this page for comments)

THE HISTORY OF ACID TRIPPING

NOTES

(Please use this page for comments)

THE HISTORY OF ACID TRIPPING

MIKAZUKI PUBLISHING TITLES

Adventures of Jasper

Arctic Black Gold

The Bribe Vibe

Find the Ideal Husband

Learning Magic

Mikazuki Jujitsu Manual

Magic as Science & Religion

Karate 360

25 Principles of Martial Arts

Letting the Customers Win

Political Advertising Manual

Political Candidates Manual

Living the Pirate Code

Small Arms & Deep Pockets

World War Water

THE HISTORY OF ACID TRIPPING

More Titles Coming Soon
Visit www.MikazukiPublishingHouse.com
for more information on our books.

Mikazuki Publishing House is a book
publishing house specializing in a variety
of fiction, non-fiction, and Childrens
books.

Press Contacts interested in arranging
press interviews and/or author
appearances, are welcome to contact:

pr@MikazukiPublishingHouse.com

We believe that the written word is

THE HISTORY OF ACID TRIPPING

the most effective vehicle for the

delivery of knowledge and that reading

is essential to educating oneself.

Mikazuki Publishing House believes in

the promotion of reading as a tool for

self progression and therefore invests

resources, working with libraries and

institutions of higher learning, to

propagate the advantages of reading.

Mikazuki Publishing House is honored

to be an active participant in the fight to

reverse world deforestation.

Approximately 30 million trees are

cut down in the U.S. every year to be

used for the creation of print books. We

THE HISTORY OF ACID TRIPPING

wish to offset and counterbalance the

use of paper in the book publishing

industry by working with organizations

dedicated to reversing the trend of world

deforestation. We will first start with one

tree.

The consequences of not doing so could

be disastrous for future generations.

Every minute, over 160 acres of

land feel the destructive effects of

deforestation. Deforestation causes

species to become extinct, disrupts

natural habitats, and erodes the top soil of

viable farming lands causing drought

and famine.

THE HISTORY OF
ACID TRIPPING

As a responsible book publisher,

Mikazuki Publishing House will donate a

percentage from the sale of each book

to the effort of planting millions of trees.

Mikazuki Publishing House is

pleased to invite foundations,

associations, and groups dedicated to

planting trees to contact us.

Please send all requests to:

philanthropy@MikazukiPublishingHou
se.com

Mikazuki Publishing House enables

greater exchange of knowledge by

providing our authors to public

institutions as guest speakers.

As our authors have limited time

THE HISTORY OF ACID TRIPPING

due to writing and book tours, we ask

that you submit a request outlining the

type of event with its pertinent

information included.

We invite requests from the following types

of organizations:

Public Libraries/Book Fairs

Event Management organizations

Community Centers

Community Colleges/Universities

Book Clubs with over 50 Active members

Please send all requests to:

philanthropy@MikazukiPublishingHouse.com

Mikazuki Publishing House is a proud

THE HISTORY OF ACID TRIPPING

member of the Independent Book

Publishers Association

"EDUCATION IS THE KEY TO HAPPINESS"

KAMBIZ MOSTOFIZADEH

www.ingramcontent.com/pod-product-compliance
Lightning Source LLC
Chambersburg PA
CBHW050533280326
41933CB00011B/1576